*ar
*eagle's
of
irish
lighthouses

GW00391634

*john *eagle *

An eagle's view of irish lighthouses

Published by Eagle's Eye Publications
Eyeries, Beara, Co. Cork, Ireland

International Standard Book Number

0 9537271 0 6

Printed by: CIT brace harvatt

Design and production:
Peter Williams Associates 01646 698825

contents

1

foreword

To many people lighthouses are special places. Their function, architecture, and isolation sets them apart. Over the centuries lighthouse technology has progressed from coal or wood fires to solar-powered energy-efficient electric lights. Yet their purpose remains constant - the safety of life at sea.

As the era of full-time lighthouse keepers vigilantly tending the light through the hours of darkness has come to an end, there has been an enormous rise of interest in lighthouses by members of the public.

John Eagle's Irish Lighthouse series of picture post cards have given great pleasure to many and are much sought after by lighthouse enthusiasts worldwide. Now he has assembled a further collection of his photographs and written his own account of the lighthouses pictured. I am pleased to have been invited to write the foreword to this book which, I am sure, will be greatly appreciated.

T.M. Boyd
Chief Executive
The Commissioners of Irish Lights

Introduction

Lighthouses have long been an obsession of mine. They hold a certain magical atmosphere and taking photographs of them is something I have enjoyed time and again. Since 1994 I have been turning my photographs into postcards. Many people who contact me either through magazines or over the Internet have asked how they can get to see some of the lighthouses. So I have decided to write this guide, to tell lighthouse enthusiasts how they can get to the lighthouses on the Irish coast. While a lot of these lighthouses are best viewed from helicopters there are still a great many that can be reached by boat or on foot. I hope you enjoy this book and take it with you as you explore the beautiful Irish coastline.

A couple of things to remember, a good pair of walking boots are essential. Also be wary of the cliffs, many are highly dangerous and close to these lighthouses. I would also ask you to remember to leave farm gates as you find them, either open or closed.

Note: Please take care when visiting any of Ireland's lighthouses, as many are located in hazardous places. Most of Ireland's lighthouses are the property of the Commissioners of Irish Lights, 16 Lower Pembroke Street, Dublin. Unless written permission has been given by them in advance please don't enter the actual premises of any of the lighthouses unless under the guidance of an Attendant. River Shannon lighthouses Beeves Rock and Tarbert are owned by Shannon Estuary Ports at 3 Pery Square, Limerick.

I wish to thank the Commissioners of Irish Lights for their invaluable help; Michael Costeloe for his lighthouse history information; Capt. Mick Conneely and Capt. Mick Hennessy of Irish Helicopters for their assistance in getting me to and from the lighthouses. I also wish to thank the following for their very kind assistance over the years. Tom MacSweeney of RTE; Marine Times Newspapers of Killybegs, Co Donegal; Sue Hill; Ken Trethewey; Peter Williams; Luke O'Brien; Jimmy Dowds; Bill Britten; Linda Anderson, Barney Whelan, Jennifer Henderson and Kathy Finnegan.

how to get there

County Dublin - pp7-11
Lighthouses: Howth, Baily, Dun Laoghaire east and west.
This lighthouse journey starts at Dublin, and follows the coast around southward; this is a rough guide on how to get to each county, detailed instructions to get to each lighthouse are on the following pages. Positions are given in lat and long; also, for the Irish Discovery map series, available from bookshops, the approximate number has been given. Please check before you buy!

County Wexford/ County Waterford - pp12-21
Lighthouses: Tuskar, Rosslare Harbour, Hook Head, Dunmore East, Ballinacourty, Mine Head.
Head south along the coast from Dublin.
From Cork: head north east following signs for Waterford via Youghal.

Co. Cork - pp22-42
Lighthouses: Charles Fort, Old Head Kinsale, Galley Head.
From Cork head south, taking the road to the Airport, and follow signs to Kinsale. You can get to Galley Head driving from Kinsale on the Timoleague road; alternatively, take the N71 via Bandon to Clonakilty where you look for signs to Galley Head or Ardfield.
Lighthouses: Spit Bank, Roches Point, Youghall, Ballycotton.
Take the Waterford road out of Cork; refer to directions on relevant pages.
Lighthouses: Fastnet, Mizen, Sheep's Head, Copper Point, Crookhaven, Barrack Point.
From Cork city take N22, following signs for Killarney. Approx. ten miles after Ballincollig, turn left at signpost for Castletown Bearhaven (also spelt Castletownbere). 2 miles on turn left at Crookstown and follow signs for Dunmanway. Here, take R586 towards Bantry; after 15 - 20 miles look for a sign pointing left to Ballydehob. Take this and go to Schull.
Lighthouses: Roancarrigmore, Ardnakinna, Bull Rock, Calf Rock.
Follow directions to Crookstown as above, then turn left and follow signs to Castletown Bearhaven; be careful not to go to Dunmanway. Follow signs for Kealkil, then Ballylickey; turn right here for Glengarriff, then left at Glangarriff Post Office to go down the Beara Peninsula.

Places I recommend to stay in at:
Wicklow: Wicklow Head Lighthouse, available from The Irish Landmark Trust, Dublin. 353 (0) 1 670 4733
Adrigole: The Carey Co. Irish Rentals (these are houses to rent by the sea) http://www.irishrentals.com fax: 027 60244; Hungry Hill Lodge, Hostel and Camping, tel/fax 027 60228.
Castletownbere: Ford Ri Hotel: 027 70379; The Old Presbytery, 027 70424.
Eyeries area: Coulagh Bay B&B, 027 74013; Foromanes House, 027 74360; Sea Front, 027 74198; Anam Cara Writer's and Artist'sRetrat 027 74441.

Goleen: The Heron's Cove B&B and Restaurant, *Fresh Fish and Wine on the Harbour.* Open all year round. Tel: 028 35225; Fax 028 35422; email: suehill@tinet.ie ; The Lobster Pot, great for a drink.

County Kerry - pp43-48
Lighthouses: Skellig Michael, Cromwell Point, Inishtearaght, Little Samphire Island, Tarbert.
Co. Kerry is in the south west of Ireland: if landing at Shannon head for Limerick and drive south; if landing at Cork drive west, following signs for Killarney.
Lauragh: Caha Mountain Holidays, 064 83108; Cummers Cottage 064 83934.

County Clare - pp50-57
Lighthouses: Beeves Rock, Scattery Island, Kilcredaune, Loop Head, Blackhead.
If landing at Shannon, leave the airport and turn left for Ennis on N18. Then follow directions given for the respective lighthouses. For Limerick leave the airport and turn right. The dual-carriageway will take you to Ennis or Limerick.

Aran Islands, Co. Galway - pp58-64
Lighthouses: Inisheer, Straw Island, Eeragh.
If landing at Shannon leave the airport, turn left and drive north to Ennis, then follow signs to Doolin where a ferry will take you to the islands, or continue north to Galway where you can fly to the islands, or take R336 from Galway to Rossaveel where a ferry will take you to the islands. Please check beforehand on times of ferries. Galway Tourist Office phone number is: 091 563081

County Mayo - pp66-70
Lighthouses: Blackrock Mayo, Blacksod, Broadhaven, Eagle Island.
Mayo is in the west of Ireland, north west of Galway, due south from Donegal. From Galway follow signs for Westport, then north to Belmullet. If travelling from Donegal follow signs to Sligo, then to Ballina and on to Belmullet.

County Sligo - pp73-76
Lighthouses: Metal Man Sligo, Oyster Island, Blackrock Sligo.
From Galway head north on N17 through Tuam, Knock, Tobercurry to Sligo. From Dublin take the N4, passing through Mullingar, Longford, Carrick on Shannon and so on up to Sligo. From Donegal town head south on N15.

County Donegal - pp77-84
Lighthouses: St John's Point, Rotten Island, Aranmore, Tory Island, Fanad.
From Dublin take the N4 to Sligo, then head north on N15. The road runs up beside the coast to Donegal town where you will either turn left for lighthouses Rotten Island and St. Johns, or continue north for Fanad and Tory Island.

Postcards in the Irish Lighthouse Series that show the lighthouses mentioned in this guide: (* taken from helicopter)

1: Roancarrig
2C: Fastnet*
3A: Fastnet*
4: Galley Head
5: Old Head
6B: Mizen*
7A: Ardnakinna*
8: Bull Rock*
9: Skellig Michael
10: Inishtearaght*
11: Cromwell Point*
12: Roches Point
13: Ballycotton
14: Youghal
15A: Hook Head
16: Crookhaven
17A: Ardnakinna*
18: Calf Rock*
19A: Skellig Michael*
20: Cromwell Point
21: Little Samphire Is.
22: Tarbert

23: Loop Head
24A: Crookhaven*
25A: The Baily
26A: Kilcredaune
27A: Scattery Island
28A: Roche's Point
29: Ballinacourty
30A: Inishtearaght*
31A: Beeves Rock
32A: Bull Rock*
33A Mine Head
34: Sheeps Head*
35: Spitbank
36: Metal Man Sligo
37: Oyster Island
38: Eeragh*
39: Straw Island*
40: Blackhead
41: Inishmore*
42: South Rock ALF
43: Howth (new)
44: Howth (old)

45: Dun Laoghaire (east)
46: Dun Laoghaire (west)
47: Copper Point
48: Charles Fort
49A: Barrack Point
50: Sheeps Head
51A: Tory Island*
52: Fanad*
53: Rotten Island
54: St. Johns (Donegal)
55: Helicopter at Fanad
57: Blacksod
57A Blacksod*
58: Broadhaven
59: Blackrock*
59A: Blackrock*
60: Eagle Island*
61: Dunmore East
61A   "   " (close up)
62: Rosslare Harbour
63: Tuskar

Below: *The author, John Eagle, in his studio. Photograph Niall Duffy.*

✳ CO ✳ ᴅUBᴌIN ✳

Howth
Baily
Dublin
Dun Laoghaire (east
Dun Laoghaire (west

howth (new)

Nearest Town: Howth
Location:
>**Lat/Long:** 53°23.6N 006°04.0W
>**Irish Discovery Series:** 50

How to get there: Take the DART from Dublin City heading north. The old traditional tower and tall modern lighthouses are both on the East Pier at the entrance to Howth harbour.

Lighthouse Details

Established: 19 May 1982
Structure: White concrete
Elevation: 13m
Range: W17nm R15nm
Character: Gp fl (2) WR 7.5 s

Above: The new light is at the end of teh pier.
Left: The old lighthouse was established 1 July 1818. The adjoining living quarters were started in 1821. The keepers had been living in the tower until then. It was discontinued 19th May 1982 when replaced by the new automated tower.

8

the Baily

Nearest Town: Howth
Location:
      Lat/Long: 53°21.7N 006°03.1W
      Irish Discovery Series: 50
How to get there: Take the DART from Dublin city heading north. On leaving the station turn right and go up the hill as if heading back towards Dublin. The way to the lighthouse is off to the left, on one of the smaller roads. It is not easy to find but anyone local will be able to tell you. The lane will open out onto a large grassy expanse. Follow the lane to the gates; you will not be able to enter, however a good, distant view of the lighthouse can be had.

Lighthouse Details

Established: 17 March 1814　　　　**Range:**　　27nm
Elevation:　41m　　　　　　　　　　**Character:**　fl W (20 sec)
Structure:　Granite tower, white buildings (white tower until 1910)
Demanned: 24 March 1997

ꝺun laoghaire [east anꝺ west]

Nearest Town: Dun Laoghaire
Location:
    Lat/Long: (east) 53°18.1N 006°07.6W
                (west) 53°18.2N 006°07.8W
    Irish Discovery Series: 50

How to get there: Take the DART from Dublin city heading south. Follow directions to the harbour; most obvious will be the Seacat ferry buildings that take passengers across to Holyhead in Wales. The lighthouses are on opposite sides of the harbour. After walking up to the West Pier light, the East Pier light can be seen across the harbour.

Next to the ferry buildings is the Commissioners of Irish Lights Depot, which often has buoys in the yard for overhaul. Sometimes there will be a lightfloat (automated light vessel) in the harbour either awaiting dry-docking and refit, or transfer to a new station after refit. It may have SOUTH ROCK or CONINGBEG painted on its side. If the vessel is awaiting refit, this will indicate its last station. If the refit has been completed, it will be the station the vessel is going to next.

The name of the station is not the same as the name of the vessel, which, of course, does not change. The three lightfloats currently in service are named Gannet, Kittiwake and Skua.

Lighthouse Details

Established:
 East 1 Oct. 1847
 West 24 Sept. 1852
Elevation:
 East 16m
 West 11m
Range:
 East 22nm
 West 7nm
Character:
 East Fl(2)W 15s
 West Fl(3)G 7.5s
Automated:
 East 1 Sept. 1977
 West 1930

Right: Dun Laoghaire East.

Below: Dun Laoghaire West. Original F R character changed to Fl R 10s in 1930; 1933 changed again to present characteristic.

11

✳ CO ✳ WEXFORD ✳

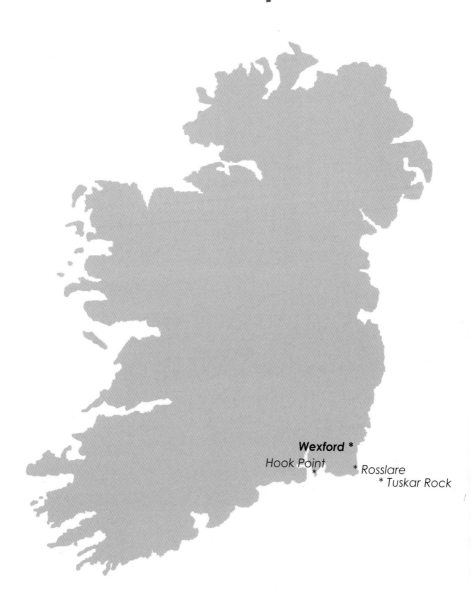

Wexford ✳
Hook Point
✳
✳ *Rosslare*
✳ *Tuskar Rock*

tuskar

Nearest Town: Rosslare
Location:
    Lat/Long: 52°12.2N 006°12.4W
    Irish Discovery Series: 77
How to get there: Situated on dangerous rocks 7 miles off the south-east coast of Ireland, Tuskar is best viewed by helicopter, or on one of the ferries that sail from Rosslare to Fishguard or Pembroke.

Lighthouse Details

Established: 4 June 1815
Structure: White tower
Range: 27nm
Automated: 31 March 1993

Engineer: George Halpin
Elevation: 33m
Character: Q(2)W 7.5s
Helicopter reliefs started Jan. 1975.

Tuskar was the third lighthouse on the coast to be converted to electric.

ROSSLARE HARBOUR

Nearest Town: Rosslare
Location:
   Lat/Long: 52°15.4N 006°20.2W
   Irish Discovery Series: 77
How to get there: It is on the end of the Ferry Port railway line that runs along the breakwater pier.

Lighthouse Details

Structure: Red metal tower
Elevation: 15m
Range: W13nm R10nm G10nm
Character: LFl WRG 5s

hook head

Nearest Town:
Location:
    Lat/Long: 52°07.3N 006°55.7W
    Irish Discovery Series: 76
How to get there: From Waterford go to the Passage East Ferry, then on the Wexford side of the river follow the signs for Hook Head.
From Wexford follow signs to Passage East Ferry, looking out for signs to Hook Head pointing to your left.
On your way back from the Hook, why not stop by at Templars Inn; your host is Jimmy Cullen, who used to be in the lighthouse service, and his pub is a treasure trove for enthusiasts. It is also a warm and welcoming place for a meal and a drink.
(Tel 051 397162)

Lighthouse Details

Established: circa 1172
It is one of the oldest lighthouses in Europe. Originally it was looked after by monks. The present optic was installed in 1910, and the lighthouse was converted to electricity on 1 August 1972.
Structure:
White tower, two black bands.
Elevation: 46m
Range: 23nm
Character: Fl W 3s
Automated: 29 March 1996

⁕ CO⁕WATERFORD ⁕

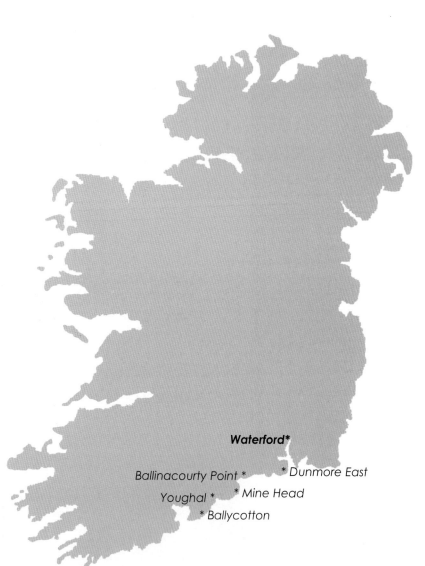

Waterford*

Ballinacourty Point *   * Dunmore East

Youghal *   * Mine Head

* Ballycotton

ᎠᴜNᴍᴏʀᴇ ᴇᴀsᴛ

Nearest Town: Dunmore East
Location:
      Lat/Long: 52°08.9N 006°59.3W
      Irish Discovery Series: 76
How to get there: From Waterford head south. The lighthouse is sit-
uated at the end of the breakwater pier of this charming harbour.

Lighthouse Details

Structure:
      Grey granite tower,
      white lantern

Elevation:
      13m

Range:
      W16nm R12 nm

Character:
      LF1 WR 8s

Demanned:
      15 June 1922

Ballinacourty

Nearest Town: Dungarvan
Location:
    Lat/Long: 52°04.7N 007°33.1W
    Irish Discovery Series: 82

Lighthouse Details

Established:
  1 July 1858
Structure:
  White limestone tower
Elevation:
  16m
Range:
  W12nm R9nm G9nm
Character:
  Fl(2)WRG 10s
Electrified:
  12 Feb. 1964

Present apparatus was installed in 1929

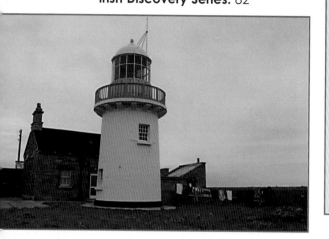

How to get there: This lighthouse can be seen from afar, and can be maddening to reach by car. However, it is possible. As you approach Dungarvan on the N25 from Waterford, look for the signs for the Gold Coast Hotel or Gold Coast Golf Club. Follow these until the hotel, after when the road takes a sharp left. At the next T junction take a right. The lighthouse is about half a mile down that road on the right hand side. Once you get there you will see that your journey was really worthwhile, as this is a charming place.

mine head

Nearest Town: Dungarvan
Location:
      Lat/Long: 51°59.6N 007°35.2W
      Irish Discovery Series: 82

How to get there: Heading south from Dungarvan on the N25, after about 10 miles look for a small whitewashed pub called Flemings on your left, at the junction of the N25 and D53. Turn left here, pass the pub, continue through the next crossroads until you come to a church and school on the left. A little further on you will find John Paul's bar; continue until you see a new factory on your left, and stop at the crossroads 100 yards on. Turn right at the Post Office, heading downhill towards the sea. Take the second road to the left; it is a narrow lane serving two houses and the lighthouse. You are looking for a farm with a cattle grid at the entrance and a red sign that says 'Slow", and a green danger sign saying 'Do not Approach' and mentions heavy machinery. Just beyond these signs is a bungalow; please stop here and ask for permission to proceed to the lighthouse. Be advised that you are entering private property; please do not park your car in the lane as it will cause an obstruction to local farmers. The cliffs by the lighthouse are high and steep - please be careful.

Lighthouse Details

Established:	1 June 1851
Engineer:	George Halpin
Structure:	White tower, black band
Elevation:	87m highest in Ireland
Range:	28nm
Character:	Fl(4)W 20s
Electrified:	8 Sept. 1964

youghal

Nearest Town: Youghal
Location:
     Lat/Long: 51°56.5N 007°50.5W
     Irish Discovery Series: 81/82

How to get there: Driving from Dungarvan into Youghal you will see it ahead of you before reaching the main part of the town. It is right beside the main road on the site of an old convent.

Lighthouse Details

Established:
  1 February 1852
Structure:
  White granite tower
Elevation:
  24m
Range:
  W12nm R9nm
Character:
  Fl WR 2.5s
Electrified:
  1964
Demanned:
  21 December 1939

20

Ballycotton

Nearest Town: Ballycotton
Location:
    Lat/Long: 51°49.5N 007°59.1W
    Irish Discovery Series: 81

How to get there: Drive south from Youghal towards Cork until you reach Castlemartyr. Follow the signs from here to Ballycotton. The lighthouse is on an Island just off the shore. To see it properly ask on the pier if there is a local boat owner who would be willing to take you for a trip around the island.

Lighthouse Details

Established:	1 June 1851
Structure:	Black tower and lantern, enclosed in white walls
Elevation:	59m
Range:	W22nm 18nm
Character:	Fl WR 10s
Automated:	1992
Electrified:	1975

The original 1851 optic was replaced by an AGA sealed-beam lamp array in 1975.

✳ CO ✳ CORK ✳ SE ✳

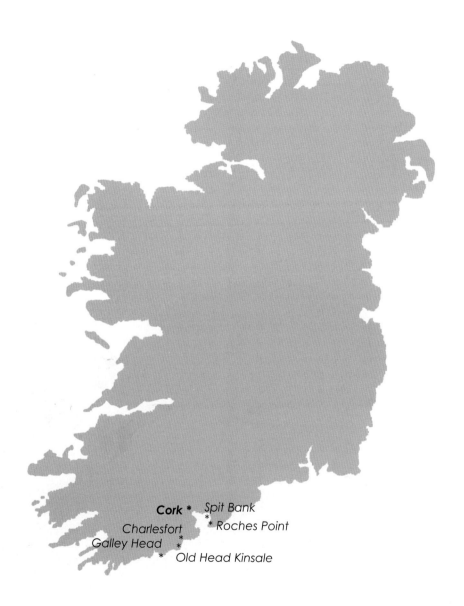

Cork *   * Spit Bank
                   *
Charlesfort   * Roches Point
Galley Head *
              *   Old Head Kinsale

Charles Fort

Nearest Town: Kinsale
Location:
    Lat/Long: 51°41.7N 008°29.9W
    Irish Discovery Series: 89
How to get there: From Kinsale follow the directions to Charles Fort. These will take you up and around the harbour, the road is often narrow. The best way to see the lighthouse is to go into the fort, where a small admittance is charged. This is well worth paying as the fort is impressive.

Lighthouse Details

Built:
    1804 although a light has been lit in a window since the 16th Century.
Established:
    27 April 1929
Structure:
    Lantern on SW rampart of fort
Elevation:
    18m
Range:
    W9 nm R6nm G6nm
Character:
    Fl WRG 5s

roches point

Nearest Town: Whitehead
Location:
>**Lat/Long:** 51°47.6N 8°15.3W
>**Irish Discovery Series:** 81

How to get there: Drive south from Youghal towards Cork until you reach Midleton. Turn off and follow the signs for Whitehead. From Whitehead keep on the main road; there is a turn off to the right rising steeply to a large industrial complex. Do not turn up this road; instead, take the next turn off to the right. Follow to the end and you will rise up over the crest of a hill and the lighthouse will come into view.

Lighthouse Details

Built: 1835 when the original tower, deemed to small for Cork Harbour, was dismantled and taken to Duncannon.
Structure: White tower
Elevation: 30m
Range: W20nm R16nm
Character: Oc WR 20s

spitвank

Lat/Long: 51°50.7N 008°16.4W
Irish Discovery Series: 81/87

How to get there: Drive from Cork City heading east on the new link road, following signs for Cobh. In Cobh it can be seen from the waterfront with a good pair of binoculars. Ask on the pier if there is a local boat owner who would be willing to take you out there.

In 1848 the Ballast Board received a letter from the Cork Harbour Commissioners urging them to replace one of their buoys where the channel turns through just over 90°. After much correspondence the Board agreed to the request and decided to place one of Alexander Mitchell's patent screw pile structures on the spot. Mitchell's tender was accepted in February 1851, and work went ahead over the next two years. A dioptric 6th order fixed red light was changed in 1877 to incorporate a 24° white sector light which pointed north-east over Bar Rock. This sector was increased to 25° in 1903. A fog bell introduced in 1895 sounded twice every 30 seconds and was discontinued 5 March 1985. Deterioration of the wooden decking and superstructure was detected in 1958; by 1963 steel replacements had been added. The structure was seriously damaged 17 December 1978 when MV Levensau dragged her anchor. Spitbank was handed over to Cork Harbour Commissioners 1 November 1985.

Lighthouse Details

Established: 1 March 1853
Structure: White house on red piles
Range: W10nm R7nm

Engineer: Alexander Mitchell
Elevation: 10m
Character: Iso WR 4s

old head kinsale

Nearest Town: Kinsale
Location:
Lat/Long: 51°36.3N 008°31.9
Irish Discovery Series: 89
How to get there: From Kinsale drive south; the road will take you over the river and approximately 2 miles later you will see a sign pointing to Old Head. Follow this road to a large tower and some gates, which may be closed. A golf course has been built there and you might not be allowed to enter. Shortly before the gates you should be able to see the lighthouse.

Lighthouse Details

Built:
1850
Established:
1 October 1853
Engineer:
George Halpin
Structure:
Black tower, two white bands
Elevation:
75m
Range:
25nm
Character:
Fl(2)W 10s
Automated:
1987

This is one of the oldest lighthouse locations in Ireland, dating back to beacons in pre-Christian times. The remains of the first lighthouse proper can still be seen. Sir Robert Reading was granted permission by King Charles 2nd to have a cottage style lighthouse 13 November 1665. It had an open coal fire brazier on its roof. In 1804 the Revenue Commissioners, responsible for lighthouses on the coast outside Dublin, instructed their contractor for lighting, Mr Thomas Rogers, to construct a temporary six foot diameter lantern with 12 oil lamps and reflectors to replace the coal fire on the roof.

In July 1812 George Halpin reported the poor state of the temporary light and recommended a more permanent fixture. 3 months later sanction was obtained to build a new light, similar in design to the Baily. It cost £9,500 to build and a fixed white light was established 16 May 1814, 294 feet above high water. It comprised of 27 Argand oil lamps each with its own parabolic reflector and could be seen in clear weather for 23 miles.

However in 1844 the Elder Brethren of Trinity House reported that like Cape Clear the lighthouse was too high and often obscured by low cloud. Inspector Halpin agreed and on 20th March 1850 he marked out the new site. 15 months later the tower was 60 foot high, dwelling half built and the compound wall almost complete. The new station was completed 1853 at a cost of £10,430. A fixed white light was lit 236 feet above high water. The 100 foot cut stone tower was plastered on the outside from ground to balcony and painted white with two red bands. This colour scheme was changed in 1930 to its present black and white tower.

galley head

Nearest Town: Rosscarbery
Location:
      Lat/Long: 51°31.7N 008°57.1W
      Irish Discovery Series: 89
How to get there: From Skibbereen drive east to Rosscarbery, and, passing the town on your left, cross the new road bridge and after a mile or so take the turn on your right for R598. This will take you along beside the coast, lots of beaches and sand dunes, and you will see the lighthouse a few miles away if you stop anywhere here. Continue on up a steep hill, through what looks like a farm, then at the top you will come to a crossroads with cul-de-sac sign ahead of you. Turn right here and follow the road until you can go no further, the lighthouse will be ahead of you.

Lighthouse Details

Established:	1 January 1878	**Structure:**	White tower
Elevation:	53m	**Range:**	27nm
Character:	Fl(5)W 20s	**Automated:**	1979

*Cork

hakinna   Roancarrigmore
Bull Rock * *
              Sheep's Head
Calf   *   Barrack Pt
Mizen Head   *
              ** Copper Point
              Crookhaven
              Fastnet

BARRACK point

Nearest Town: Baltimore
Location:
   Lat/Long: 51°28.3N 009°23.6W
   Irish Discovery Series: 88
How to get there: Either follow directions from Baltimore to the beacon and view the lighthouse across the harbour's mouth, or take the ferry from Baltimore pier to Sherkin Island. Once there, walk up the hill and turn to your left. A pleasing walk of approx. one or two miles brings you to the lighthouse. If you choose to visit Baltimore Beacon, please be wary of the very sheer cliffs.

Lighthouse Details

Established: January 1886 after the Commissioners of irish Fisheries asked the Commissioners of Irish Lights in 1882 to look at the possibility of a light on the southern entrance to Baltimore Harbour. In 1884 the Rev. Charles P. Davies, Chairman of the Skibbereen and Baltimore Harbour Board, asked the Commissioners of Irish Lights to exhibit a small guiding light. The fixed red and white light character was changed in 1978.
Structure: White tower
Elevation: 40m
Range: W6nm R3nm
Character: Fl(2)WR 6s
The light is maintained by the Baltimore Harbour Commissioners.

copper point

Nearest Town: Schull
Location:
      Lat/Long: 51°30.2N 009°32.0W
      Irish Discovery Series: 88
How to get there: From Bantry take the R586 south. Approx. 5 miles from the town centre turn right to Ballydehob. On reaching the village turn right for Schull. Take the coast road from Schull and after a mile Long Island will come into view. Copper Point Lighthouse is on the island; it can clearly be seen with the naked eye, however, binoculars or a telephoto lens would be useful.

Lighthouse Details

Built: 1864 as unlit beacon
Light est.: 1 June 1977
Structure: White round tower
Elevation: 16m
Range: 8nm
Character: Q(3)W 10s

Designated as a lighthouse in 1981

CROOKhaven

Nearest Town: Goleen
Location:
> **Lat/Long:** 51°28.6N 009°42.2W
> **Irish Discovery Series:** 88

How to get there: The best vantage point to see this lighthouse is on the hill beyond the village of Crookhaven, where you can also see the Fastnet. The other way is not so easy and you may well be stopped as it is a private access road. From Goleen follow signs for Crookhaven; look out for a sign pointing left for Rock Island where the lighthouse is situated. The road is narrow, high walled, and very difficult to turn a car around in. I recommend continuing to Crookhaven and the hill after the village.

Lighthouse Details

Established:	1 August 1843	**Structure:**	White granite tower
Elevation:	20m	**Range:**	W13nm R11nm
Character:	LFl WR 8s	**Demanned:**	17 February 1911

fastnet

Nearest Town: Crookhaven
Location:
>**Lat/Long:** 51°23.3N 009°36.1W
>**Irish Discovery Series:** 88

How to get there: From Bantry drive south. Passing the Westlodge Hotel on your left, continue on the main road until the ESSO station, then take the right turn a couple of hundred yards after it. Follow signs for the Mizen until Goleen; then keep to the coast road ignoring Mizen signs. Follow signs to Crookhaven which will take you on a big loop around the harbour. There are several places to view the Fastnet on the way; however, close viewing is not possible without boat or helicopter. Ask on the pier at Crookhaven, or Baltimore or Schull for a boat owner willing to take you there. Another option is to take the ferry from Baltimore to Cape Clear Island.

Lighthouse Details

Built:
>1899 - 1903

Structure:
>Grey granite tower replacing the original of 1854, the remains of which can still be seen.

Elevation:
>49m

Range:
>28nm

Character:
>Fl W 5s

mizen

Nearest Town: Goleen
Location:
   Lat/Long:
   51°26.9N 009°49.2W
   Irish Discovery Series: 88

How to get there: Follow signs as given for Fastnet; once in Goleen follow the signs to Mizen. There is a telecottage in Goleen dealing specifically with the Mizen, and the staff there will be happy to advise you. Open to the public since 1994, a visit to Mizen begins with a walk across the suspension bridge which spans the gorge, and gives a valuable insight into how light stations were run, with guided tours of the lighthouse, and video of early helicopter reliefs. A full history of the Mizen is on show with numerous old pictures showing it being built.

Lighthouse Details

Established:
   Fog signal 1909;
   radio beacon 1931;
   light 1959
Structure:
   Concrete platform
   and lantern
Elevation:
   55m
Range:
   16nm
Character:
   Iso W 4s
Automated:
   1 April 1993

sheep's head

Nearest Town: Kilcrohane
Location:
Lat/Long: 51°32.5N 009°50.8W
Irish Discovery Series: 88

How to get there: From Bantry as you pass the West Lodge Hotel on your left look for a turning to your right that goes to Sheep's Head. This will take you along the scenic south side of Bantry Bay. Alternatively, take the road just past the ESSO station as for the Mizen, but turn right at the post office at Durrus and follow signs for Kilcrohane. Go through the village and on for another 4 or 5 miles. No caravans or trailers are advised as the road is very narrow and twisty, and at one point doubles back on itself. The road ends at a car park where refreshments are available during the summer. Leave your car here and walk the remaining 1 or 2 miles, without dogs, please, as the local farmers are concerned for their sheep. Please take note of the danger signs regarding cliffs on this awe-inspiring walk, which is part of the Sheep's Head Way route opened by President Mary Robinson in 1996.

Lighthouse Details

Established:
14 October 1968 primarily for oil tankers passing to and from Whiddy Island oil storage tanks. Helicopter and donkey transported materials and equipment to the site.

Structure:
white

Elevation:
83m

Range:
W18nm R15nm

Character:
Fl(3)WR 15s

ROANCARRIGMORE

Nearest Town: Castletownbere
Location:
>**Lat/Long:** 59°39.1N 009°44.8W
>**Irish Discovery Series:** 85

How to get there: Another one for helicopter or boat. 7 miles drive from the Supervalu in Castletownbere on the Adrigole road there is a small layby. With binoculars or a telephoto lens the lighthouse can be seen. Alternatively drive east from Castletownbere by about 2 miles and go down to the pontoon for Bere Island near the golf course. Take Patrick Murphy's ferry across to Lawrence Cove, then walk up to the village and turn left. Keep walking as far as you can (it's up to you) and the lighthouse will be ahead of you. On the way back why not stop at Kitty's cafe for a lovely welcome and a great meal.

Lighthouse Details

Built: 1847 by Mr Howard of Limerick	**Engineer:** George Halpin
Structure: White round tower, black band	**Elevation:** 18m
Range: W18nm R14nm	**Character:** Fl WR 3s
Demanned: 23 September 1975	

ardnakinna

Nearest Town: Castletownbere
Location:
    Lat/Long: 51°37.1N 009°55.0W
    Irish Discovery Series: 88/84
How to get there: Take the ferry from the slip in Castletownbere to the western end of Bere Island. Make your way up from the pier to the T junction, follow the Beara Way signs that go to the west of the island; the Way passes by the lighthouse. Be careful; the cliffs are highly dangerous.

Lighthouse Details	
Built: Originally an unlit beacon in 1850	**Elevation:** 62m
Est.: Light 23 November 1965	**Range:** W17nm R14nm
Structure: White round tower	**Character:** Fl(2)WR 10s

BULL ROCK

Nearest Town: Allihies
Location:
      Lat/Long: 51°35.5N 10°18.1W
      Irish Discovery Series: 84
How to get there: Follow directions as for the Calf; turn through 90° at the ruin to view Bull Rock. Binoculars or a telephoto lens would come in handy for a clearer view.

Lighthouse Details

Established:	1 January 1889, replacing the Dursey island light which was set up after Calf Rock was destroyed.
Structure:	White tower
Elevation:	83m
Range:	23nm
Character:	Fl W 15s
Fog Signal:	explosive replaced with a three-trumpet siren operated by air compressors 1 April 1902; discontinued 17 May 1989
Conversion:	from oil-gas to vapourised paraffin 28 June 1910
Helicopter reliefs:	started 1969
Electrified:	21 August 1974
Automated:	March 1991

Calf Rock

Nearest Town: Allihies
Location:
    Irish Discovery Series: 84
How to get there: From Castletownbere drive west towards Allihies. 9 miles or so on this road you will see a turn off to Dursey Island. Follow this road to the cable car parking area at the end; take the cable to Dursey and walk to the end of the island. Here you will find the old lighthouse ruin that was temporarily constructed 2 Feb. 1882 after the Calf Rock light was destroyed by a violent storm. An old lightvessel lantern was used atop a three-roomed structure. From this vantage point you will see Calf Rock ahead.

Lighthouse Details

Built:
    1861 - 1864 by Henry Grissell of Regent's Canal Iron Works, London. The lantern, optic and revolving machinery were added in 1865.
Established:
    30 June 1866
Elevation:
    41m (tower 36m high)

Shore dwellings for the keepers and their families were built on the mainland near Dursey Sound. A savage storm in the first part of 1869 washed the away parts of the lantern balcony rail and a store hut. The keeper on shore thought he saw distress flags, and so, with 6 boatmen, rowed out only to find the keepers safe and sound. When the boat began to return to the mainland it was caught by the sea and all hands were lost.

During 1870 the tower's base was strengthened, the diameter increased from 20 to 312 feet. A cast iron skirt was added and the space between filled with rubble.

The lighthouse was destroyed by a violent storm on 27 November 1881; for two weeks the keepers and three other men were trapped on the rock before being helped ashore by the boat attendant working in conjunction with HMS Seahorse.

✳CO✳KERRY✳

Tarbert *

Little Samphire Island
*
Inishtearaght
*
Cromwell Point   * **Killarney**
* Skellig Michael

skellig michael

Nearest Town: Port Magee
Location:
     Lat/Long: 51°46.2N 010°32.5W
     Irish Discovery Series: 83

How to get there: There are numerous boat operators ready and willing to take you out to the rock from Port Magee and Ballinskelligs. The lighthouse is not particularly easy to view. When on Skellig Michael, climb up to Christ's Saddle, then go up to the left towards the towering finger of rock. Be aware that this viewing point is highly dangerous as the ground falls away steeply to the ocean. The lighthouse can be seen from this vantage point. A safer way to view the light is to go around the rock by boat; the Skellig Experience vessel is one such.

Lighthouse Details

Built:	Originally two lights, upper and lower, both 4 Dec. 1826
Established:	Present (lower) light 25 May 1967, after extensive rebuilding and modernisation. Temporary light was mounted nearby during rebuilding, from 24 May 1966 - 25 May 1967. Upper light was discontinued when Inishtearaght was built in 1870.
Structure:	White tower
Elevation:	53m
Range:	27nm
Character:	Fl(3)W 10s
Demanned:	22 April 1987

cromwell point

Nearest Town: Knights Town, Valentia Island
Location:
> **Lat/Long:** 51°56.0N 010°19.3W
> **Irish Discovery Series:** 83

How to get there: From Killarney take the north shore drive on the Ring of Kerry to Cahirciveen. Pass through the town and after about a mile follow the signs to Port Magee. Cross over the bridge, then turn right and drive to Knights Town.

Lighthouse Details

Established: 1 February 1841		**Structure:**	White tower
Elevation: 16m		**Range:**	W17nm R15nm
Character: Fl WR 2s		**Automated:** 4 November 1947	

inishteaRaght

Nearest Town: Dunquin
Location:
      Lat/Long: 52°04.5N 010°39.7W
      Irish Discovery Series: 70
How to get there: Drive west from Dingle on the Slea Head drive. You will see the towering pyramid-like rock, but the lighthouse itself will remain hidden as it is on the far side of the island. The best way is to view from a helicopter, but a local boat owner from Dingle or Dunquin should be able to take you there.

Lighthouse Details

Established:	4 May 1870, after 5 years of rock blasting and building
Structure:	White tower
Elevation:	84m
Range:	27nm
Character:	Fl(2)W 20s

Westernmost of the Blasket Islands; known to many as The Tearaght.

tARBERt

Nearest Town: Tarbert; under control of Shannon Estuary Ports
Location:
   Lat/Long: 52°35.5N 009°21.8W
   Irish Discovery Series: 63/64
How to get there: Best seen from the car ferries that regularly cross the Shannon at this point. The lighthouse stands on Electricity Supply Board (ESB) property. There is a security guard stationed at the entrance who might let you take a quick picture.

Lighthouse Details

Established:
   31 March 1834
Structure:
   White round tower
Elevation:
   18m
Range:
   W14nm R10nm
Character:
   Iso WR 4s
Demanned:
   1 April 1919
Electrified:
   8 December 1966

Four changes have been made to the optic: first in December 1871 when it was changed from catoptric to dioptric; second in May 1905 from fixed light to Iso W 2s; third change to acetylene was postponed in 1914 due to the war, eventual conversion was effected on 1 April 1919 using a water to carbide generating plant; the fourth and present light is electric, similar to other minor lights around the coast, using a cluster of three 100W Argenta type lights.

In the event of electricity failure a standby 3Kw diesel alternator automatically takes over, and if that fails, the Attendant fits a cluster of seven 20 litre acetylene burners which run off an AK25 cylinder.

Right: *The 200ft (61m) cast-iron footbridge was not constructed until 1841.*

The lighthouse was handed over to Limerick Harbour Commissioners (now Shannon Estuary Ports) 1 January 1981.

little samphire island

Nearest Town: Fenit
Location:
> **Lat/Long:** 52°16.2N 009°52.9W
> **Irish Discovery Series:** 71

How to get there: From Tralee follow signs to Fenit; drive to the pier and just before there are places to park. From there a pleasant walk can be had along the beach on a footpath. At low tide it is possible to walk out almost as far as the lighthouse, but be warned not to be cut off by the incoming tide!

Lighthouse Details

Established: 1 July 1854	**Structure:** Blue round stone tower
Elevation: 17m	**Range:** W16nm R13nm G13nm
Character: Fl WRG 5s	**Demanned:** 5 December 1954
Electrified: 28 October 1976	

*CO*CLARE*

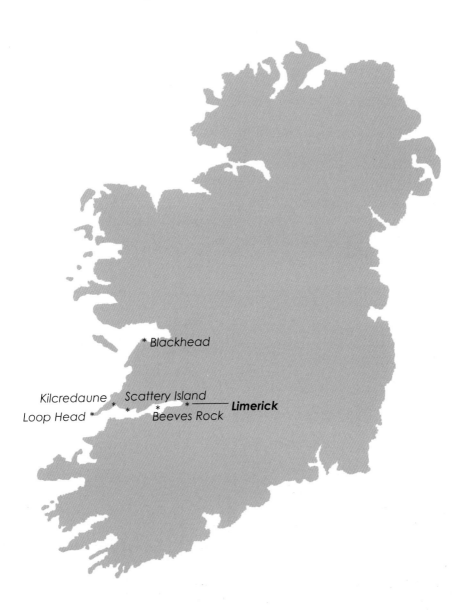

*Blackhead

Kilcredaune   Scattery Island
Loop Head *   *   *   * ———— **Limerick**
                      Beeves Rock

BEEVES ROCK

Nearest Town: Foynes
Location:
  Lat/Long: 52°39.0N 009°01.3W
  Irish Discovery Series: 64
How to get there: To see it properly you need to hire a boat. From Tarbert drive east towards Limerick to Askeaton; Foynes is halfway between Tarbert and Askeaton. If coming from Limerick take N69 to Askeaton,then head north to the Shannon. At Foynes there is a museum dealing with the old Trans-Atlantic flying boats; possibly they will know how to get out to the lighthouse. I went with Shannon Workboats from the Aughinish Pier which is on private property; however, their number is in the directory.

Lighthouse Details

Established: May 1855	**Engineer:** George Halpin
Elevation: 12m	**Range:** W12nm R9nm
Character: Fl WR 5s	**Demanned:** 11 February 1933
Structure: Dark stone-coloured tower	

In October 1812 the Limerick Chamber of Commerce requested that a perch be placed on Beeves Rock. The Board agreed as long as the cost did not exceed £20. After 16 months of deliberation it was decided a more substantial building was required. and by early 1816 a tower had been completed with an outside stone stairway leading to a door into a room under the roof. It was anticipated that the tower could later be converted into a lighthouse. Pointing and whitewashing was completed by May 1816. In 1846 Lord Mounteagle of Mount Trenchard, Foynes, applied for a lighthouse on the north point of Foynes Island. The Board and the Limerick Chamber of Commerce decided between them that Beeves Rock would be the best position for a light. Converting the tower into a lighthouse was abandoned in favour of a plan by George Halpin to build a dwelling adjoining the lighthouse to save the high cost of housing keepers ashore. In March 1848 the contract to build was awarded to Mr William Burgess. Due to the adverse tidal conditions building was slow, 8 foot of water covered the rock at high tide. and it wasn't until 1851 that the building was completed. The lantern dome, 3rd order dioptric apparatus and general completion took a further four years. In May 1855 a fixed light showing white to the south, red to the north was established. Sited at mouth of River Fergus, 2.5 miles from the Aughinish buoy, it came under jurisdiction of Limerick Harbour Commissioners Jan 1st 1981, now Shannon Estuary Ports.

Below: Scattery Island

scattery island

Nearest Town: Kilrush
Location:
      Lat/Long: 52°36.3N 009°31.0W
      Irish Discovery Series: 63/64
How to get there: From Ennis follow signs for Kilrush on N68.
From Tralee drive north on N69 to Tarbert, then take ferry across
the Shannon and turn left for Kilrush. Head for the harbour where
there are boat trips to the island.

Lighthouse Details

Established:
    December 1872, present
    apparatus 1993
Structure:
    White tower
Elevation:
    15m
Range:
    10nm
Character:
    Fl(2)W 7.5s

Originally the lighthouse was designed to be on rails so it could be moved when the nearby fort had firing practice.

It was destroyed by a storm in 1868 six months into being built.

The light guides shipping into the River Shannon.

loop head

Nearest Town: Kilkee
Location:
> **Lat/Long:** 52°33.7N 009°55.9
> **Irish Discovery Series:** 63

How to get there: As for Kilrush and Scattery; at Kilrush turn right for Kilkee where you make a left for Loop Head on R487. The light is situated at the mouth of the River Shannon. Please be advised if taking small children that while the land surrounding the lighthouse looks great for playing on, the cliffs are unprotected and very dangerous. There is a small area to park cars outside the lighthouse gates.

Lighthouse Details

Established: Original cottage-type light 17th century; present light 1 May 1854.

Structure:	White tower	**Elevation:**	84m
Range:	28nm	**Character:**	Fl(4)W 20s
Electrified:	1971	**Automated:**	March 1991

kilcredaune

Nearest Town: Kilkee
Location:
> **Lat/Long:** 52°34.8N 009°42.5W
> **Irish Discovery Series:** 63

How to get there: From Ennis follow signs for Kilrush; on N68 turn right for Kilkee where you make a left for Loop Head on R487. 4 to 5 miles from Kilkee look for signs pointing left for Carrigaholt, R488. (There is a turning for Carrigaholt shortly after leaving Kilrush, avoiding Kilkee, but it tends to be bumpy in places and is mostly single track.) From the village follow the Loop Head Drive sign; you will come to a straight stretch of road with a right hand bend. The sign will point you around the bend, instead drive straight ahead towards a very unusual Swiss-looking wooden chalet. Close to it you will see bright yellow signs indicating private property; this is the entrance to Kilcredaune. When I went there in April 1999 the lady told me she did not mind visitors coming to the lighthouse as long as they signed the visitor's book, which I willingly did. Please make yourself known to her or her son upon arrival.

Right: The dog on the stairwell is Quisha, the author's faithful collie.

Lighthouse Details

Built:	1854
Structure:	White tower
Elevation:	41m
Range:	13nm
Character:	Fl W 6s
Demanned:	1931; also tower truncated
Electrified:	1979

Blackhead

Nearest Town: Ballyvaghan
Location:
   Lat/Long: 53°09.2N 009°16.0W
   Irish Discovery Series: 51
How to get there: From Galway drive south on the N18, follow signs for Kinvara, then Ballyvaghan, and proceed along the coastal road. It will be on your right.

From Limerick head north on N18, turn off at Ennis on N85 for Ennistimon, then Lisdoonvarna and turn left for the Burren and follow the coast north. The lighthouse is situated on the northern extremities of the Burren.

Lighthouse Details

Established:
   21 February 1936
Structure:
   White tower
Elevation:
   86m
Range:
   W22nm R16nm
Character:
   Fl WR 12s

✻aran✻islands✻
✻co✻galway✻

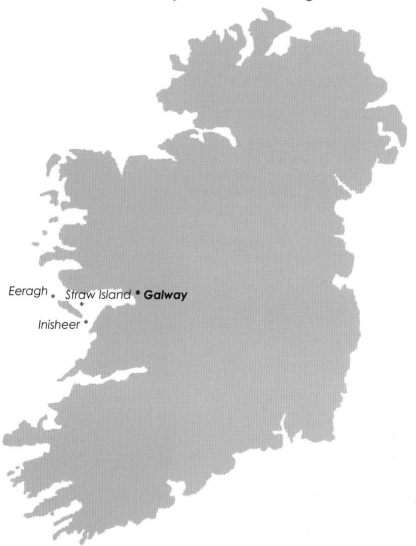

Eeragh ✻   Straw Island ✻ **Galway**
        ✻
    Inisheer ✻

inisheer

Nearest Town: Inisheer
Location:
      Lat/Long: 53°02.8N 009°31.5W
      Irish Discovery Series: 51

How to get there: From Limerick head north to Ennis, drive through the town until you reach a roundabout, take the first left and follow the signs for Ennistimon N85.   There is a turn0off to Lisdoonvarna, R47, which you can take, then R476. Alternatively drive to Ennistimon and then head to Lisdoonvarna from there. Just outside Lisdoonvarna turn left for Doolin, where there are supposedly 'millions of signs' for the ferry; if, like me, you can't see any signs, turn left at the crossroads and head towards the coast, making a right soon afterwards.   The pier has plenty of car parking space, and a ferry runs May to September. Buy your ticket, yellow for Inisheer, at the booking office, and the ferry journey takes about 30 minutes. The lighthouse can be seen to your left as you near the island, and if you time it right, you should be able to get a shot of it with an old wreck nearby. On landing at the pier there awaits an assortment of pony traps and tractor-driven touring buses to take you around the island. If you decide to walk then turn left, follow the shore until you pass a school playing field on your right, then look for the narrow lane leading up the hill between two fair sized castles. Keep walking between brilliantly constructed stone walls and, after cresting the hill, you will see the lighthouse ahead of you.

Lighthouse Details

Established:	1 December 1857, the same day as Eeragh
Structure:	White tower, black band
Elevation:	34m
Range:	W20nm R 16nm
Character:	Iso WR 20s
Demanned:	3 March 1978

straw island

Nearest Town: Kilronan
Location:
      Lat/Long: 53°07.0N 009°37.9
      Irish Discovery Series: 51
How to get there: You see this lighthouse on the way to Inishmore from the mainland. Landing on the island might not be easy; ask on the pier at Rossaveel for a local boat owner who would be willing to take you out there. There are regular passenger ferries leaving Rossaveel for the Aran Islands; also from Doolin and Galway.

Lighthouse Details

Established: 1 September 1878	**Structure:** White tower
Elevation: 11m	**Range:** 17nm
Character: Fl(2)W 2s	
Demanned: 30 September 1926, with acetylene light	
Electrified: 23 Aug. 1980, using wind generator to charge batteries.	

eeRagh

Nearest Town: Kilronan
Location:
> **Lat/Long:** 53°08.9N 009°51.4W
> **Irish Discovery Series:** 51

How to get there: The best way is by helicopter; however, if not available, then by boat from the main island of Inishmore, or from the mainland. Planes fly to the Aran Islands from Galway; perhaps you could arrange with a pilot to give you an aerial tour. Ask on the pier at Rossaveel, R336 west from Galway town, about boat hire. There are regular passenger ferries leaving Rossaveel for the Aran Islands; also from Doolin and Galway.

Lighthouse Details

Established:
> 1 December 1857, the same day as Inisheer

Structure:
> White tower, two black bands

Elevation:
> 35m

Range:
> 23nm

Character:
> Fl W 15s

Electrified:
> 2 June 1978

Demanned:
> 21 December 1978

The most north-westerly light in the Aran chain of islands

✳ co✳mayo ✳

Eagle Island *   Broadhaven
              *
Blackrock * * Blacksod
                * *Ballina*

blackrock mayo

Nearest Town: Blacksod
Location:
    Lat/Long: 54°04.0N 010°19.2W
    Irish Discovery Series: 22/23
How to get there: From Blacksod take the road beside the post office up the hill. You will see Blackrock in the distance. The best way to view the lighthouse is by helicopter as it is in a dangerous location. Ask about a boat on the pier at Blacksod. There are boat trips to the islands just off the coast, so an excursion to Blackrock might be possible.

Lighthouse Details

Established:
    1 June 1864
Structure:
    White tower
Elevation:
    86m
Range:
    W20nm R16nm
Character:
    Fl1 WR 12s
Demanned:
    Nov 1974

On the 3 August 1999 a new solar-powered light was exhibited during the hours of darkness. While ths was being fitted a temporary light, exhibiting a reduced range, was put in place on 12 July.
The 1st Order dioptric was ordered from Chance Brothers in Dec. 1861, the lantern from Neilkins. Stored in Belmullet Nov 1862 due to bad weather

Blacksod

Nearest Town: Blacksod
Location:
> **Lat/Long:** 54°05.9N 010°03.6W
> **Irish Discovery Series:** 22/23

How to get there: From Sligo follow the signs to Ballina, then Belmullet and approximately 12 miles further is Blacksod.
From Westport drive north to Belmullet. The lighthouse is on the pier and easy to view.

Lighthouse Details

Established: 30 June 1866	**Structure:**	White lantern on dwelling
Elevation: 13m	**Range:**	W12nm R9nm
Character: Fl(2)WR 7.5s	**Demanned:**	1931
Electrified: 31 May 1967	**Light system:**	3x100W Argenta lamps

---

Helicopter base for Blackrock and Eagle Island lighthouses. Originally mentioned by Lieutenant Nugent of the Coast Guard who wrote a letter in 1841, forwarded to the Board by Mr James Dombrain, Inspector General of the CG. In June 1861 the Inspecting Committee recommended placing a light on Blacksod Point which would, in conjunction with Blackrock, make Blacksod Bay a safe anchorage. An inspection that

took place on the 8 and 9 June 1863 agreed that a lighthouse be built near Blacksod pier, (known locally as Termon pier,) not the actual Blacksod Point which is approx. 1.6km to the sw. Plans were submitted in September 1863 by JS Sloan, the Board's Superindent of Works and Foreman, and were sent to Mr CP Cotton, the Board's Consulting Engineer, who approved the design. Four tenders for building were received, and Mr Bryan Carey put forward the winning bid of £2,100. The lighthouse was built using red granite from a local quarry, brought to the site on a tramway system.

BROADHAVEN

Nearest Town: Belmullet
Location:
      Lat/Long: 54°16.0N 009°53.3W
      Irish Discovery Series: 22/23
How to get there: From Belmullet drive west for approx. a mile then turn right. Head north, then east; you are aiming for the harbour where the lifeboat is kept. There is a high wall here. Park the car and look over the wall, and you will see the lighthouse to the north, accessible after a pleasant walk. Please be aware that the surrounding area can fall away steeply in places.

Lighthouse Details

Established: 1 June 1855	**Structure:** White tower
Elevation: 27m	**Range:** W12nm R9nm
Character: Iso WR 4s	**Demanned:** 1 December 1931

Sited on Gubacashel Point, Broadhaven Light guides vessels from seaward clear of a sunken rock on the western side of Broadhaven into safe anchorage. A light or beacon was first looked for by the Coast Guard in 1843; engineer George Halpin reported that if a lighthouse was not approved then a beacon tower could be built with floors and steps so that at a later date it could easily be altered into a lighthouse. The fixed third order dioptric lens was supplied by W Wilkins of London, showing white to seaward and red to the west. In 1931 the colour of the tower was changed from natural grey stone to white; the candlepower was increased to 3000, then 4000 in 1946.

69

eagle island

Nearest Town: Belmullet
Location:
      Lat/Long: 54°17.0N 010°05.5W
      Irish Discovery Series: 22/23
How to get there: I flew to Eagle Island by helicopter; however, I believe you can get a reasonably good view from the land if you drive west from Belmullet and make a right a short distance from the town. Head north, then northwest for the coast.

Lighthouse Details	
Established:	29 September 1835
Structure:	White tower
Elevation:	67m
Range:	26nm
Character:	Fl(3)W 10s
Electrified:	17 July 1968
Automated:	1988
Helicopter relief:	Began 1969

In 1830 applications were made to the Ballast Board by Commanders Blake and Glascock of the Coast Guard Service for a light on Blackrock or Inishmann Point. Mr G. Halpin, the Board's Inspector however reported in favour of Eagle Island, one of the most storm battered islands on the Irish coastline. It is close to the Continental

70

Shelf. Keepers and Attendants talk of hearing the rush of the wave surge coming towards the island before it strikes.

It was agreed to build two lighthouses on the island in 1830, Eagle Island West and Eagle Island East. The base of the West Tower was 196 feet above high water and during construction a great sea swept the partly built tower, two courses high, and much of the building materials clear into the sea. The two towers were finally completed and a massive storm wall was built on the sea side of the towers.

The towers, 64 feet and 87 feet high were 132 yards apart with their lanterns at the same level 220 feet above high water. When the two lights at night, or towers in daytime, were in line they guided vessels past all the dangers from Blacksod Bay to Broadhaven including the Stags.

Four months after first being lit, on January 17th 1836, the lantern of the West Tower was struck by a rock which shattered one of the panes of glass and extinguished the light for an hour. The Keepers' dwellings were badly damaged, and in those days their families lived with them.

Both lanterns were badly damaged by a violent gale on the 5th and 6th February 1850.

On March 11th 1861 at midday the light room of the Eastern Tower was struck by sea smashing 23 panes, washing some of the

Right: Note the massive walls to protect against storms.

Above: *Remains of the old discontinued, storm-ravaged east lighthouse.*

lamps downstairs, and damaging the reflectors with broken glass beyond repair. Truly an incredible wave to have come up 133 feet of rock, and then a further 87 feet of lighthouse tower to cause so much damage. So much water cascaded down into the tower that it was impossible for the Keepers to open the door. They had to drill holes to let the water out first. In spite of efforts by the Keepers it wasn't until the night of the 12th before the light was restored, and then only with 12 lamps and reflectors.

The storm that struck Eagle Island on the 29th December 1894 damaged the dwellings of the East Station beyond repair. It also broke the lantern glass, put out the light and damaged the protecting wall. The families took shelter in the tower and it was not until the next day that the families at the West Tower heard of their friends' plight. East Tower was discontinued 1895.

⁕ CO⁕SLIGO⁕

Blackrock
Metal Man
Sligo
Oyster Island

metal man, sligo

Nearest Town: Rosses Point, Sligo
Location:
  Lat/Long: 54°18.2N 008°34.5N
  Irish Discovery Series: 25
How to get there: Drive north from Sligo town, following signs for Rosses Point. The Metal Man is within easy viewing distance from the shore, although a good pair of binoculars would come in handy. Turn through 90° and you will also see Blackrock lighthouse out in the bay.

Lighthouse Details

Established: on Perch Rock as the Metal Man Beacon in 1921
Structure: Statue of man on a tower
Elevation: 3m
Range: 7nm
Character: Fl W 4s

The Metal Man, the same as the one at Tramore, Co. Waterford, was originally going to be put where the Blackrock lighthouse now stands, but when the merchants of Sligo looked for Blackrock (then a beacon) to be converted to a lighthouse, the sailor, on their suggestion, was placed on Perch Rock. An acetylene light was established beside him 6 October 1908, and was converted to propane 9 October 1979.

oyster island

Nearest Town: Rosses Point, Sligo
Location:
Lat/Long: 54°18.1N 008°34.2W
Irish Discovery Series: 25
How to get there: Drive north from Sligo town following signs for Rosses Point. As you drive towards the end of the road you will see the lighthouse on your left.

Lighthouse Details	
Established:	1 August 1837
Structure:	Tower
Elevation:	13m
Range:	10nm
Character:	Oc W 4s

Two lights were established at the same time, forming leading lights from Sligo Bay into the channel to Sligo Port. Replaced by a sectored temporary light 15 February 1891. Discontinued towers taken down 1893. North tower was rebuilt and became a rear leading light with the Metal Man. Light converted from acetylene to propane 9 October 1979.

blackrock, sligo

Nearest Town: Rosses Point
Location:
       Lat/Long: 54°18.4N 008°37.0W
       Irish Discovery Series: 25
How to get there: Drive north from Sligo town, following signs for Rosses Point. Passing Oyster Island lighthouse on your left continue on for another half mile; the road curves sharply to the right. Outside the big hotel turn left and you will see the lighthouse out in the bay. For a closer look you can make your way to Coney Island, or go down to the pier at Rosses Point and find someone with a boat who would be willing to take you out into the bay. Please don't walk from Coney Island to the lighthouse; for one thing you will be entering private property, and also you might be cut off by the tide.

Lighthouse Details	
Established:	**Converted from unlit beacon in 1835**
Structure:	White tower, black band
Elevation:	White light 24m, Red light 12m
Range:	White light 13nm, Red light 5 nm
Character:	White light Fl W 5s, Red light Fl R 3s
Demanned:	November 29 1934

This lighthouse contains two separate lights; the red flashes over Wheat and Seal Rocks, visibility 107° - 130° (23°).

✳co✳donegal✳

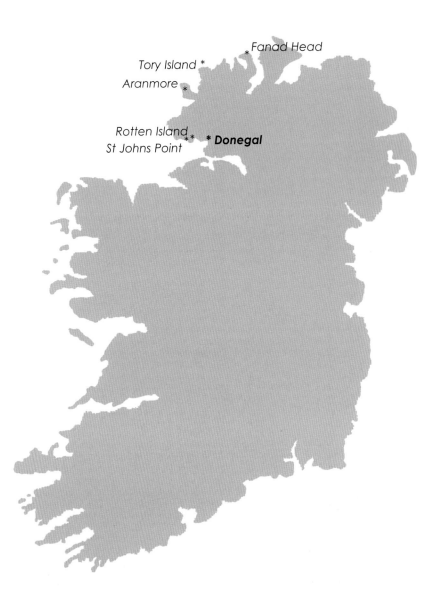

Fanad Head *

Tory Island *

Aranmore *

Rotten Island **
St Johns Point * **Donegal**

st Johns point

Nearest Town: Killybegs
Location:
      Lat/Long: 54°34.2N 008°27.6W
      Irish Discovery Series: 44/45
How to get there: Take road out to Donegal town passing through Bruckless; 1.5km after Bruckless on the main road keep an eye out for signs for Castlemurray House Hotel and Restaurant. Take a right turn here and this road will carry you out to the point; a straight enough road but very long and narrow.

Lighthouse Details

Established:	4 November 1831
Engineer:	George Halpin
Structure:	Granite, white tower
Elevation:	30m
Range:	14nm
Character:	Fl W 6s
Demanned:	1930s
Electrified:	1962

The final cost of the lighthouse at the end of 1833 was over £10,000. Just over a hundred years later the fixed catoptric light was changed to a first order cylinder refractor occulting 4s light, 2s dark, and used acetylene generated from carbide instead of oil. 1 July 1942 light character changed from occulting to a flash of 2s every 6s. The duration of the flash was reduced from 2s to 1.5s 1 February 1965.

rotten island

Nearest Town: Killybegs
Location:

> **Lat/Long:** 54°36.9N 008°26.3W
> **Irish Discovery Series:** 44/45

How to get there: Take the road to Donegal town past the Fish Meal go over the bridge and take the first right after the bridge. This road will bring you across a very narrow bridge and then its a twisty road past some very very big houses and a nursing home, and its straight out to the point looking over at Rotten Island (about a 10 min. drive).

Lighthouse Details

Established: 1 September 1838
Engineer: George Halpin
Structure: White tower
Elevation: 20m
Range: W15nm R11nm
Character: Fl WR4s
Demanned: 7 January 1959
Electrified: 1 February 1963

First requested by Mr Drury, Inspecting Commander of the Coast Guard, 21 april 1832, suggesting the light should be put on Drumanoo Point. George Halpin agreed that a light was necessary, but recommended Rotten Island at the entrance to Killybegs harbour. The lighthouse, made of cut granite, originally showed a a fixed white light visible for 12 miles. In 1910 the light was changed to a 5th order dioptric flashing W3s. This character altered 1 February 1965 to the present fl WR4s.

ARANMORE

Nearest Town: Leabgarrow
Location:
    Lat/Long: 55°00.9N 008°33.6W
    Irish Discovery Series: 22
How to get there: Head west from Letterkenny, or north-west from Killybegs, to Burtonport where a ferry will take you across to Aranmore. The crossing takes about 25 minutes and passes through numerous small islands and rocks making a pleasing journey. The ferry takes cars, and runs on a regular basis throughout the year; the operator can be contacted on 075 20532.

On reaching the island drive a short distance along the harbour then turn right and proceed up the steep hill. A mile or so up the hill and you will reach a staggered cross; you need to go straight on which involves a turn to the right and then left. Continue on this road past a small lake and out to the lighthouse where there is parking space outside the gates. Please note that the cliffs are sheer, and at one point fall away close to the road so caution is advised.

Lighthouse Details
Built:
1804
Structure:
White tower
Elevation:
71m
Range:
29nm
Character:
Fl(2)W 20s
Demanned:
1 August 1976
The light was discontinued between 1838 and 1865.

tory island

Nearest Town: West Town
Location:
  Lat/Long: 55°16.4N 008°14.9
  Irish Discovery Series: 1
How to get there: Take N56 north from Letterkenny until you see a sign for Meenlaragh on R257, where a ferry will take you to Tory Island. There is a nice hotel on Tory. At night the island is graciously swept over by the lighthouse beam. The walk to the lighthouse from West Town will take you half an hour to an hour, depending on the strength of the wind. It is an open area with little shelter.

Lighthouse Details	
Established: August 1832	**Structure:** Black tower, white band
Elevation: 40m	**Range:** 30nm
Character: Fl(4)W 30s	**Automated:** April 1990

The light ran on oil until a small gasworks was built nearby. Coal gas was used until conversion to vapourised paraffin in 1923. Electrified in 1972.

fanad

Nearest Town: Letterkenny
Location:
      Lat/Long: 55°16.6N 007°37.9W
      Irish Discovery Series: 2
How to get there: Drive north on R245. Look out for signs for Portsalon on R246. Shortly before Portsalon turn left for Fanad.

Lighthouse Details

Established:	17 March 1817
Structure:	White tower
Elevation:	39m
Range:	W18nm R14nm
Character:	Fl(5)W 20s
Automated:	1975

Fanad is the helicopter base for Tory Island and Inishtrahull. It was first lit after the frigate *Saldana* was wrecked there in 1812. A fixed catoptric light showed red to sea, white to Lough Swilly, visible for 14 miles. 12 August 1909 a new revolving 3rd order lens was installed. The apparatus was completely replaced when light was automated.

postcaRδs available fRom...

Dublin
Maritime Museum in Dun Laoghaire (complete series).   Greene's Bookshop.

Wexford/Waterford
Waterford: Christchurch 2000. **Dunmore East:** Dingley's.

County Cork
Cork: The newsagents in Princes Street, (Large selection of my cards). **Glengarriff:** The Spinning Wheel and the Post Office.   **Adrigole:** Peg's Shop. **Castletownbere:** Murphy's Supervalu; The Shell Craft Shop (large selection of my cards); Donegan's; The Old Bakery (great place for a meal); McCarthy's Pub (great place to have a drink); John Murphy, Churchgate. **Bere Island:** The Post Office; Kitty's Cafe.   **Eyeries:** The Post Office; Donal Houlihan's; O'Sullivan's Supermarket. **Allihies:** The Post Office;   John Terry's. **Ardgroom:** The Post Office. **Goleen:** Mizen Vision! **Baltimore:** The Post Office; Cotters. **Crookhaven:** O'Sullivans. **Bantry:** The Gift Shop; Swains. **Kilcrohane:** The Post Office. **Durrus:** O'Briens. **Healy Pass:** Don's Cabin.

County Kerry
Lauragh: The Post Office; The Keeper's Cottage; Robert O'Shea up near the sawmills.   **Tarbert:** Post Office.   **Kenmare:** Foley's Craft Shop.   **Port Magee:** Post Office. **Dingle:** Sammy's on Inch Strand; Dunquinn Pottery at Slea Head, (nice place to have a meal). There are lots of interesting pictures on the walls of the Blaskets, and the film 'Ryan's Daughter' was made in the area.

Aran Islands
Kilronan: Heritage Centre, island of Inishmore.

County Clare
Kilrush: Finucans in Frances Street. **Carrigaholt:** the pub/shop on the corner as you come in from Kilkee. **Kilbaha:** the pub/shop nearest the pier.

County Mayo
Belmullet: Post Office. **Blacksod:** Post Office.

County Sligo
Rosses Point: Doherty's.

County Donegal
Tory Island: Maureen Rodgers.   **Fanad:** Post Office up near Fanad.

Unless stated, these outlets only sell cards of their particular area. Complete series available from The Lighthouse Depot in Maine, USA, and Dave Long, Modern Postcard Sales, P.O. Box644, Elkhart, IN 46515, USA. A good selection can be had from Trinity House Lighthouse Museum in Penzance, Cornwall, and Mizen Vision! near Goleen.
Leading Lights, Milford Marina, Milford Haven, SA73 3AF UK

✦ index ✦